FRONTIER TO TOP TIER

A Photo Retrospective from The Dallas Morning News and its Readers

DMN Archives

Published by Pediment Publishing, a division of The Pediment Group, Inc., www.pediment.com. Printed in Canada.

Preface

What began as a settlement in 1841 has grown into a metroplex, now the fourth-largest metropolitan area in the country.

What began as a small-town newspaper on Oct. 1, 1885, has grown into a multimedia company whose news and information are consumed around the globe by more than a million people every day.

One thing that remains unchanged over the course of 125 years is our understanding that we must earn our readers' trust. We must show, every day, that our news reports have no agenda but the truth. That we are not beholden to any elected official, political party or political ideology. That we report

as forthrightly about the powerful as about the powerless, acting neither from fear nor favoritism nor malice. This is a great responsibility, and we approach it with determination and humility.

The founder of *The Dallas Morning News*, George Bannerman Dealey, summed up our mission so well that his words are chiseled in stone on the front of our building:

"Build *The News* upon the rock of truth and righteousness, conducting it always upon the lines of fairness and integrity, and acknowledge the right of the people to get from the newspaper both sides of every important question."

I want to express my gratitude to everyone who turns to us for their news and information needs. Your loyalty informs and sustains us.

I hope you enjoy this photographic history of our city and our region as seen through the eyes of *The Dallas Morning News* and its readers.

James M. Moroney III
Publisher/CEO
The Dallas Morning News

James M. Moroney Jr. (from left), Joe M. Dealey, and H. Ben Decherd stand before the portrait of their grandfather, George Bannerman Dealey, on Feb. 22, 1952, the day they were elected to the board of directors of A. H. Belo Corporation.

Foreword

When Dallas in 1841 was nothing but a primitive campsite, its founder, a wandering Tennessean, was the solitary inhabitant. Dreams of a growing town raced through his head as he looked at the muddy Trinity River from what today is Dealey Plaza.

In these early days, the key for growth was good transportation, invariably a navigable waterway. One day, founder John Neely Bryan hoped, the Trinity would link his envisioned settlement to Galveston, the Gulf of Mexico, and beyond.

Despite heroic efforts through many years, his dream would never be realized. But developing new transportation would be a key element to making isolated Dallas grow and prosper.

Bryan's place profited from its location at a natural crossing point on the river and also the area's rich black soil, good for growing crops. That advantage was not exclusive. Other towns, such as McKinney, Hillsboro, Temple, Waco and Corsicana, had the same advantage.

At first, even Mustang Branch (today's Farmers Branch) was bigger than Dallas. Dallas jumped ahead after its election in 1850 as county seat. As late as 1858, McKinney was bigger. In 1870, Collin County had more people than Dallas County. But by 1880, both Dallas and Dallas County held substantial population leads that would never be threatened. Why?

The answer is the now-classic story of Dallas enterprise. Ambitious town leaders, supported by the general population, persuaded two railroads to change their routes so that they would cross in Dallas. First came the north-south Houston & Texas Central Railway in 1872, which tied the city to the American Midwest and Northeast through a connection with the Missouri-Kansas-Texas Railroad in Sherman. The very next year, the east-west Texas & Pacific Railway arrived.

By 1885, five railroads passed through town, ensuring the city's status as the key distribution point for wholesalers. A warehouse district, predecessor to today's West End historic district, sprang up. A wave of newcomers began pouring into Dallas, especially from Tennessee, Kentucky, Missouri, Georgia and Alabama. Freed slaves and their descendants came, representing a growing portion of the population. A large number of European immigrants, landing at Galveston, headed for Dallas, many becoming important business leaders. And Mexicans, too, were attracted by the opportunities, arriving especially after the 1910 revolution.

By 1890, Dallas was the biggest city in Texas.

Local newspapers spread the word about Dallas — especially *The Dallas Morning News*, established on Oct. 1, 1885, as a branch of the *Galveston News*. From its modern plant on Commerce Street, *The News* provided the leadership needed as Dallas shed its frontier past and took on the airs of a burgeoning metropolis.

Dallas took a big step toward expanding its clout in its 1914 campaign to land a regional bank of the new Federal Reserve System. Against substantial odds, Dallas gained that designation. With an initial capitalization of $6.5 million, the bank dwarfed the combined $5 million capital of existing local banks.

Winning the bank was a signal achievement. Yet Dallas wanted more. Somehow, the city residents yearned always for greater recognition.

The Depression era offered a chance for the greatest recognition ever for the lucky city designated as host for the centennial celebration of Texas' independence. San Antonio, site of the historic Alamo, seemed a likely site. So did Houston, adjacent to the storied San Jacinto battlefield. Dallas did not even exist in 1836. What chance could it have?

Very little, except that civic ambition and energy were factors, and in that, Dallas was tops. Led by banker Robert L. Thornton and fellow bankers Nathan Adams and Fred Florence, Dallas went after the honor and won it.

More than anything, publicity preceding and accompanying the Texas Centennial Exposition of 1936 made the entire nation aware of Dallas. In retrospect, why should it be surprising that Dallas won the honor? It had achieved much the same, on a smaller scale, in 1886, when it hosted the two-day semicentennial celebration of the Texas Revolution.

Aviation's history runs deep in Dallas. The city's dedication to flight began in 1917, when leading residents implored the War Department to establish a military flying school here. They were acting on the same impulse as Bryan when he envisioned the Trinity River as the city's outlet to the world.

The War Department's answer was yes — if Dallas could secure a suitable site. Thus the committee acquired the property that became Love Field. By 1946, Love Field was the seventh-busiest airport in the nation in commercial takeoffs and landings.

Such success made Dallas refuse for years to join

hands with Fort Worth in creating a regional airport. But when federal authorities in 1964 ordered the two cities to settle on a single site, Dallas' new mayor, J. Erik Jonsson, said the time was right.

When Dallas/Fort Worth International Airport opened in 1974, it was the biggest airport in the world in land mass. It soon became one of the busiest. Largely because of the airport and its connections, nearly two dozen of the nation's Fortune 500 companies and hundreds of other businesses have their headquarters in the area. Every major city in the continental United States can be reached in four hours; almost 154,000 passengers a day arrive at or depart its terminals.

The fear of isolation that Bryan and following generations worked so hard to overcome has ended.

Darwin Payne has written eight books on Dallas history and is professor emeritus of communications at Southern Methodist University.

Acknowledgments

We greatly appreciate the work of *The Dallas Morning News* photographers past and present whose images stop time — if only for a moment.

Special thanks to Leslie White, director of photography; Irwin Thompson and Chris Wilkins, assistant directors of photography; Michael Hamtil, photo editor; Lisa Levrier, color technician; Bob Mong, editor of *The News*; John C. McKeon, president and general manager; Fran Wills, chief marketing officer; Celia Barshop, director, event marketing & promotions; Chris Henderson, segment marketer; the Dealey, Decherd and Moroney families; and our sponsor, Time Warner Cable.

Thanks to Michael V. Hazel, editor of *Legacies* regional history journal, who has written or edited 12 books on Dallas history, for crafting our chapter introductions and for sharing his expertise on short notice.

Gratitude also is due historian Darwin Payne, author of 12 books and professor emeritus of communications at Southern Methodist University, for writing the foreword and for his good-natured guidance. And to Judith Garrett Segura, retired president of The Belo Foundation and Belo historian, for her knowledge and her willingness to share it.

Without the help of Carol Roark, manager of the Texas/Dallas History & Archives Division, Dallas Public Library, and Susan Richards at the Dallas Historical Society, we would not have been able to share countless images of Dallas' rich history. Thanks also to our readers, who took the time to dig up and share their family pictures.

Laura Schwed,
editor

Linda Stallard Johnson,
copy editor

David Woo,
photo editor

Jerome Sims,
photo librarian

Contents

News Events

Since 1886, *The Dallas Morning News* has devoted much news coverage every October to the State Fair of Texas. With visiting celebrities, exhibits, and sporting events, the State Fair always has produced good stories. In 1936, the fairgrounds were overhauled to become the site for the Texas Centennial Exposition, a world's fair that ran for six months. President Franklin D. Roosevelt was among the thousands who visited the celebration of Texas' 100 years of statehood. Earlier visits to Dallas by Theodore Roosevelt (1905) and William Howard Taft (1909) also had drawn prominent news coverage. But no presidential visit, of course, left the imprint on Dallas as that by John F. Kennedy in November 1963.

The Trinity River has frequently captured the headlines, from the day in 1893 when a steamboat docked at the foot of Commerce Street after a two-month trip north from Galveston, to the great flood of 1908, the levee project of the 1930s, and, most recently, plans to transform the river with lakes, parks and other amenities.

Darker events included flu and polio epidemics, the rise of the Ku Klux Klan in the 1920s, the impact of the Great Depression, and the various wars that have claimed the lives of Dallas-area servicemen and women.

Surging urban growth has garnered headlines in recent decades with taller skyscrapers, bigger shopping malls, wider highways and new rapid-transit lines. And changing demographics resulted in African-Americans and Hispanics moving into positions of leadership.

Two weeks after Woodstock, Lewisville reluctantly hosted the Texas International Pop Festival. It was a benign skirmish in the war between the hippies and "the Establishment" during the long, hot summer of 1969 — not to mention the wildest weekend in Lewisville history. *JOE LAIRD/Dallas Morning News*

In 1876 and 1877, local businessmen sponsored Mardi Gras parades in Dallas to promote their businesses. "The festivities brought to town more people than I had imagined were in the world," said one early Dallas resident in 1876.

Below: The horse track was a big draw for the State Fair of Texas in the late 1800s. But that ended in 1903, when the state Legislature outlawed betting.

The Collections of the Dallas Historical Society

The Collections of the Dallas Historical Society

The Trinity River Navigations Celebrations took place May 4, 1893, in Dallas.

On the front page, June 29, 1886: Opening attractions at the State Fair include "Grand free barbecue."

Below: Family picnics were common at the State Fair of Texas in the early 1900s.

Henry Clogenson

DMN Archives

Boaters canoed over the flooded MK&T railyard near the Dallas Electric Light & Power plant in 1908. The Trinity River crested at a record 52.8 feet in flooding that killed five people and left 4,000 homeless; all downtown bridges were washed away.

Top: There was a lot going on at Fair Park in 1909, including free movies, a city-operated zoo, and a visit by President William Howard Taft, who delivered a speech at the racetrack.

On the front page, May 26, 1908: Flood casualties and damage are tallied.

12

Dallas City Hall was constructed in 1889 at the corner of Commerce and Akard streets at a cost of $80,000. This building was demolished 20 years later to make room for the Adolphus hotel.

The Collections of the Dallas Historical Society

Wilma Chandler

Firemen in front of the Oak Cliff station at Tenth and Tyler, 1916.

Right: Members of the Dallas Police Department lined up for a photo about 1908 outside the City Jail.

On the front page, April 16, 1912: The sinking of the Titanic.

The Collections of the Dallas Historical Society

Harry Seay of the Pacific Avenue Track Removal Committee held up the project's first pried-up spike in 1921. The removal was part of a plan to eliminate tracks on downtown streets and consolidate them into a central rail station.

On the front page, Nov. 11, 1918: World War I ends.

Walter L. Fleming Jr. sat in a goat cart in front of his house in 1923.

Left: Construction began in 1929 for the U.S. Post Office and Courthouse at Ervay, Bryan and St. Paul streets. The post office opened for business Nov. 17, 1930.

The Dallas Chamber of Commerce welcomed Charles Lindbergh (tall man in center) in September 1927.

Below: Dallas turned out for a parade for Lindbergh, who made the first solo, nonstop flight across the Atlantic the previous May.

Texas/Dallas History & Archives Division, Dallas Public Library

Natalie and George Lee

Opposite: During the Southwestern Aircraft Exposition on Oct. 11, 1927, an aerial photograph was made of Fair Park. The racetrack is at the upper left. *Carol Duff, archives Highland Park United Methodist Church*

On the front page, Oct. 29, 1929: Black Tuesday ushers in the Great Depression.

The Collections of the Dallas Historical Society

Gary Maclin

An admission ticket for the 1936 Texas Centennial Exposition.

Left: Visitors crowded the plaza in front of the Federal Building at Fair Park during the exposition.

Below left: President Franklin D. Roosevelt visited the exposition at Fair Park on June 12, 1936, and spoke to a huge crowd in the Cotton Bowl. Texas, he told his audience, was "100 years young."

The Collections of the Dallas Historical Society

Opposite: President Roosevelt (back seat on the left), next to his wife, Eleanor, traveled down Exposition Street toward the fairgrounds. The Roosevelts had just left the dedication of the Lee statue in Lee Park.

North Central Expressway under construction in 1948.

Right: Streetcars were an important form of transportation in Dallas in World War II, when gasoline was strictly rationed.

On the front page, Dec. 8, 1941: Pearl Harbor is attacked.

Texas/Dallas History & Archives Division, Dallas Public Library

President Harry Truman spoke at Burnet Field in Oak Cliff during his 1948 election campaign.

On the front page, Aug. 15, 1945: World War II ends.

Below left: Gainesville Community Circus performers and Gerry the baby elephant performed for crowds outside the Melba Theater on April 10, 1952.

Texas/Dallas History & Archives Division, Dallas Public Library

Left: A tornado struck Oak Cliff and West Dallas on April 2, 1957, killing 10 people and injuring 200. It damaged 574 buildings, most of them homes. The tornado's winds were strong enough to overturn a truck (above).

Opposite: Children from David Crockett Elementary School welcomed Fess Parker (in coonskin cap) and Buddy Ebsen (holding girl), stars of the popular TV series *Davy Crockett*, as they arrived Sept. 10, 1955, at Love Field.

CLINT GRANT/Dallas Morning News

TOM DILLARD/Dallas Morning News

Left: President John F. Kennedy and his wife, Jacqueline, greeted well-wishers at Love Field about 11:40 a.m. on Nov. 22, 1963. In the background are (from left) Nellie Connally (between the Kennedys), Lady Bird Johnson, Texas Gov. John Connally and Vice President Lyndon Johnson.

Above: Dallas turned out for the motorcade through downtown streets. "Mr. President," said Nellie Connally, in the limousine, "you certainly can't say that Dallas doesn't love you" just before the shooting that killed Kennedy and wounded her husband.

TOM DILLARD/Dallas Morning News

DMN Archives

Two days after the assassination, remembrances to the fallen president filled Dealey Plaza.

Top left: The sniper fired from a sixth-floor window of the Texas School Book Depository, looking toward the Triple Underpass.

Left: Dealey Plaza turned chaotic after Kennedy was shot about 12:30 p.m.

TOM DILLARD/Dallas Morning News

Lawmen escorted accused assassin Lee Harvey Oswald in the police headquarters garage Nov. 24 as Jack Ruby (foreground) raised a revolver to kill him. *JACK BEERS/ Dallas Morning News*

The Giant Balloon Parade, sponsored by the Dallas Chamber of Commerce, marched past the Majestic Theatre on Elm Street in 1969 to mark the start of the holiday season.

Texas/Dallas History & Archives Division, Dallas Public Library

Below left: The Rev. C.B.T. Smith and members of the Golden Gate Baptist Church held a groundbreaking ceremony about 1963.
Texas/Dallas History & Archives Division, Dallas Public Library

Below: Calvert Collins became Dallas' first female City Council member, serving from 1957 to 1961.

DMN Archives

In 1979, Lawrence Brewer returned the Ku Klux Klan hood dropped by Addie Barlow Frazier, "Kleagle of the Realm" and organizer of Dallas' first Klan march in more than 50 years.

About 300 demonstrators marched in 1978 to protest the U.S. Justice Department's refusal to pursue civil rights prosecutions in the 1973 slaying of Santos Rodriguez, 12. The boy was slain during questioning about an $8 burglary by a Dallas police officer in his squad car. More than 1,000 had marched in 1973 in a protest that turned unruly.

DAVID WOO/Dallas Morning News

Right: Sarah Weddington, an aide to President Jimmy Carter in 1979 when this photo was taken, successfully argued, at age 26, the landmark Roe vs. Wade abortion rights case before the U.S. Supreme Court. The case, decided in 1973, originated in Dallas. *JOE LAIRD/Dallas Morning News*

On the front page, July 21, 1969: Neil Armstrong takes a historic walk.

Big Tex's 8½-foot-tall boots got a touch-up for the 1990 State Fair of Texas.

Far right: President Ronald Reagan visited the Mesquite Rodeo to campaign for George Bush in 1988. George W. Bush is in the background.

IRWIN THOMPSON/Dallas Morning News

LON COOPER/Dallas Morning News

George Bush waved to the crowd in 1984 after being nominated for a second term as vice president during the Republican National Convention in Dallas.

DAVID WOO/Dallas Morning News

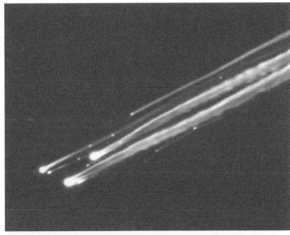

Former Dallas Cowboys players placed yellow roses by a photo of Tom Landry at the memorial service for their old coach at the Meyerson Symphony Center in February 2000.

Top left: Space shuttle Columbia disintegrated as it hurtled over North Texas on Feb. 1, 2003, killing its crew of seven.

Left: Bishop T.D. Jakes of the Potter's House in Dallas led thousands of worshipers in communion in November 2001 at the Texas Round Up for Jesus at the American Airlines Center. The service remembered those who lost their lives in the Sept. 11, 2001, terrorist attacks.

TOM FOX/Dallas Morning News

Fireworks exploded over Addison Square Circle at Addison's Kaboom Town, a daylong July Fourth celebration and fireworks show in 2004. The fireworks show was named in the Top 10 in the country by American Pyrotechnics Association.

Right: At a prayer session at the Goodwill and Salvation Army distribution center near Reunion Arena, Southern Methodist University student Daniel Liu (far left) comforted Jennifer Boudreaux, whose 22-year-old son was missing in Hurricane Katrina, while Dr. Jacqueline Lawrence (far right) of DeSoto consoled Destiny Coleman, who was searching for two brothers.

MELANIE BURFORD/Dallas Morning News

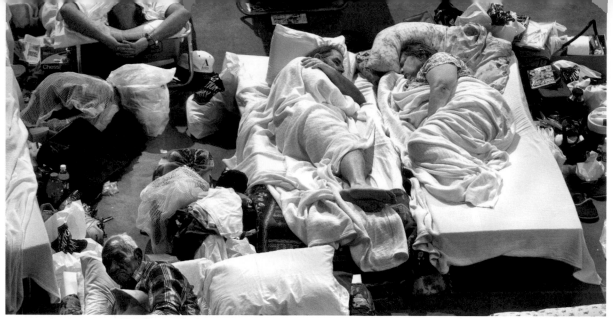

JIM MAHONEY/Dallas Morning News

Just as it was winding down from housing refugees from Hurricane Katrina, Reunion Arena took in a new group fleeing Hurricane Rita, which struck the Beaumont, Texas, area not quite a month after Katrina ravaged New Orleans in 2005.

At the Veterans Day Commemoration at City Hall in 2004, Pearl Harbor vet Houston James of Dallas embraced former Marine Mark Graunke Jr. of Flower Mound, who lost a hand, leg and eye while defusing a bomb in Iraq.

In a 2006 aerial view, marchers packed Ross Avenue downtown in support of immigration rights. *SMILEY N. POOL/ Dallas Morning News*

Top right: Lightning struck near the terminals at Dallas/Fort Worth International Airport in 2006 as an American Airlines jet took off.

Below right: A policeman stood close to danger as a fireball from Southwest Industrial Gases shot above the Houston Street Viaduct in 2007. A delivery mishap set off blasts of acetylene gas. *MICHAEL MULVEY/ Dallas Morning News*

TOM FOX/Dallas Morning News

Dut Kuol, a native of Sudan living in Dallas, held an American flag at the Martin Luther King Jr. Library in 2008 as area Darfur activists showed their support for the indictment of Omar Bashir, Sudan's president. The International Criminal Court accused Bashir of war crimes leading to the deaths of 200,000 in Darfur.

Below: Longhorns were readied for a cattle drive down Main Street that included cowboys and rodeo queens in the kickoff to the 2007 Texas Stampede and Wrangler Pro Rodeo Tour Championship at American Airlines Center.

LARA SOLT/Dallas Morning News

MONA REEDER/Dallas Morning News

The kitchen sink in a McKinney budget motel room became a makeshift tub for a 2-year-old. When the photo was taken in 2007, more than a quarter of children under age 5 in Texas lived in poverty.

MICHAEL AINSWORTH/Dallas Morning News

LARA SOLT/Dallas Morning News

JIM MAHONEY/Dallas Morning News

Mary and Chris Bush grieved for their son, Army Cpl. Peter Courcy, during his military burial Feb. 18, 2009, at Dallas-Fort Worth Cemetery. The young husband and father, 22, and another soldier died in Afghanistan eight days earlier when a car packed with explosives plowed into their Humvee.

Right: Barack Obama, then a senator, appeared at a town hall meeting at Sandra Meadows Memorial Arena at Duncanville High School on Feb. 27, 2008, while campaigning for president.

Far right below: Admirers greeted Obama after a 2008 speech at a campaign rally at Reunion Arena.

Lecia Forester (upper left) sits in front of her husband's grave at Dallas-Fort Worth National Cemetery in December 2009, two months after Jessie P. Forester Jr., a retired Army major and Vietnam veteran, died. Almost a decade after it opened, the cemetery averaged 13 interments a day, with 24,000 buried there.

VERNON BRYANT/Dallas Morning News

VERNON BRYANT/Dallas Morning News

LOUIS DeLUCA/Dallas Morning News

Texas Stadium, former home to the Dallas Cowboys football team, crumbled to rubble in an implosion on April 11, 2010.

Left: Al Rowe (with hat) and his wife, Cindy, of Wills Point took in a Blake Shelton performance from the very top row during the inaugural event June 6, 2009, at the new Cowboys Stadium in Arlington. Country superstar George Strait was the headline act, performing to 60,188 fans at the $1.15 billion venue. *TOM FOX/Dallas Morning News*

Culture

Culture in 19th century Dallas was largely imported in the form of traveling theatrical and musical troupes. Early in 1886, women organized two literary clubs (both still in existence in 2010), but the city didn't get a public library until 1901. The library included an art gallery, which evolved into the Dallas Museum of Art. Likewise, the Dallas Symphony Club, which gave its first concert in 1900, grew into today's Dallas Symphony Orchestra.

Local theater began to come into its own with the award-winning Dallas Little Theatre of the 1920s, but it took Margo Jones and her innovative theater-in-the-round productions to put the city on the national map in the late 1940s.

Following in the footsteps of earlier regionalist painters such as Frank Reaugh, the "Dallas Nine" (Jerry Bywaters, Otis Dozier, Alexandre Hogue and others) brought local art into the modern era with their depictions of the Great Depression's impact on people and of the landscape of the Southwest.

Meanwhile, in that lively, racially mixed neighborhood on the edge of downtown called Deep Ellum, Blind Lemon Jefferson attracted the notice of record producers and became the nation's best-selling African-American blues musician. New radio stations began to broadcast the blues, jazz and Western swing to listeners throughout the region.

Legendary opera diva Maria Callas launched the Dallas Civic Opera with a concert in 1957. Two years later, Paul Baker's production *Of Time and the River* opened the Dallas Theater Center. In 2010, both the Dallas Opera and DTC moved into new homes in the Dallas Arts District, joining the Dallas Symphony and the Dallas Museum of Art.

Miss Rodeo Pioneer Days 1999, Lacy Billingsley, 19, flew off a mechanical bull in the Fort Worth Stockyards in 2000. *ALLISON V. SMITH/Dallas Morning News*

Temple Emanu-El built its synagogue in 1898 at the corner of South Ervay and St. Louis, the heart of the heavily Jewish neighborhood called the Cedars.

Top: Bessie Smith was one of the blues stars who made tour stops in Deep Ellum, helping establish the section east of downtown as a blues mecca in the early decades of the 20th century.

The Social Services Sunday school class of Highland Park Methodist Church gathered at Southern Methodist University. It was the first Sunday school class formed at the church.

Below: Even in 1908, the interior of First Baptist Church was ornate. The cornerstone of the sanctuary was laid in 1891. Today, the downtown church contains seven major buildings spread over six city blocks. *The Collections of the Dallas Historical Society*

Howard Joseph Cox Sr.

Family and friends celebrated the 50th wedding anniversary of Howard and Mary Jane Webb Cox in 1912 in Dallas. From left, seated on ground, Annie Marion Cox Wilroy, Francis Howard Daniel, Rhena Merle Cox Burton, Martha Malone Elliott Rant Coonrod, Wilton J. Daniel (holding Joe Milwee Daniel), Max Alvah Daniel, Rhea Cox Daniel and Jack Lively. Second row seated, Allie May Cox, Marion Whitfield Cox, Howard Cox, Mary Jane Webb Cox, Thomas David Elliott, Mary Ross Cox Smith Elliott and Thomas Justin Cox. Third row standing, Joseph James Cox (holding Mary Frances Cox), Dorothy Adelia Martin Cox, Martha Elizabeth Cox, Alvah Harper Daniel, Sarah Olivia "Doll" Cox Daniel, Margaret Frances Cox, Mary Eleanore Harry Cox, Issac Howard Cox, Sophronia Susan Cox Lively and John T. Lively.

Full Gospel Church, an Assembly of God congregation, celebrated the first service at its new building on June 1, 1930. Even though the Rev. Albert Ott became pastor a month before Black Tuesday and the start of the Great Depression, he pushed ahead with plans to build the 1,100-seat brick church facing Peak Street.

Mary Jo Bentley

Dallas iMedia Network

Bill Camfield, better known as Icky Twerp, hosted the children's TV show *Slam Bang Theater* in the 1960s on KTVT (Channel 11), aided by his sidekick gorillas Ajax, Delphinium and Arkadelphia.

Left: Mary Jo Bentley was Queen Melody for the Centennial presentation of a pageant by 700 pupils of the instrumental classes at the Dallas public school music department in 1936.

Carrie Wagliardo Loftis

Gary W. Noe

Nathan L. Gappelberg

Nathan L. Gappelberg and Marlene Lesser went on a date to Louann's, a popular dance club on Greenville Avenue at Lovers Lane in 1949. It was billed as the largest public dining and dancing establishment in the Southwest.

The Beatles held a press conference at the Sheraton-Lincoln Hotel after a Dallas Convention Center concert in fall 1965.

Left: Jerry Haynes, who played the gentle Mr. Peppermint, gave Melvin Segroves, 4, a prize tiger and movie tickets in 1964 on WFAA-TV (Channel 8). *DMN Archives*

DMN Archives

July Fourth picnickers in 1946 enjoyed White Rock Lake near the Bath House, which was built in 1930. The Bath House reopened in 1981 as a cultural center with a 116-seat theater, gallery space and the White Rock Lake Museum.

DAVID WOO/Dallas Morning News

Patrick Duffy, who played Bobby Ewing in the TV series *Dallas*, waited for his cue on the set in downtown Dallas in 1989.

Left: The mansion of the conniving oil baron J.R. Ewing in *Dallas* was actually the sprawling home at the Southfork Ranch in Parker.

DAVID WOO/Dallas Morning News

Mick Jagger of the Rolling Stones, in the cowboy hat, performed from a cherry picker at the Cotton Bowl in Dallas on Nov. 1, 1981.

Far right: Michael Jackson sang "Another Part of Me" at Dallas' Reunion Arena, on April 25, 1988.

Opposite: Rosalinda Rios, 5, and Ricardo Garcia, 6, waited patiently for their turn to perform at the Cinco de Mayo celebration at Pike Park in Dallas on May 5, 1994.

PAULA NELSON/Dallas Morning News

DAVID WOO/Dallas Morning News

DAVID LEESON/Dallas Morning News

IRWIN THOMPSON/Dallas Morning News

John C. Hsieh

Taiwanese-American cowgirls performed at the annual convention of North America Taiwanese Women's Association in Dallas in April 2005.

Below: Anita Martinez applauded a performance by the Ballet Folklorico at the Majestic Theatre in 1999. Martinez, who served 1969-73 as Dallas' first Hispanic City Council member, founded the dance company.

HUY NGUYEN/Dallas Morning News

A child prayed with the rest of the congregation in 1997 at St. Luke Community United Methodist Church.

Right: Blues artist Buddy Ace, flanked by Little Mattie and Kay Francis, took the microphone at Longhorn Ballroom in 1991.

Kay Francis Smith

A Spotted swine was ready for its close-up in the breed demonstration area at the State Fair of Texas on Sept. 29, 2006.

Left: Ridge Lozano, 3, cries after his grandmother took the llama he was holding into the show ring without him at the State Fair on Sept. 25, 2009.

An early *Fashion!Dallas,* which was the first free-standing newspaper fashion section in the country. Introduced in June 1978, the section was widely copied by newspapers nationwide.

Far right: Kim Dawson model Karen Sexton sported athletic-inspired fashion for a May 22, 1991, *Fashion!Dallas* cover. The section covered fashion analytically and highlighted photography and graphic design.

A 2009 redesign introduced the oversize magazine format and morphed the original exclamation point into a narrow stroke.

Geof Kern

Richard Krall

EVANS CAGLAGE/Dallas Morning News

LOUIS DeLUCA/Dallas Morning News

JEFFREY PORTER/Dallas Morning News

Maestro Jaap van Zweden conducted the Dallas Symphony Orchestra on Oct. 22, 2009, at the Meyerson Symphony Center.

Left: U2 performed at Cowboys Stadium in Arlington on Oct. 12, 2009.

Left: Beyonce held a concert at American Airlines Center in Dallas on July 5, 2009.
LARA SOLT/Dallas Morning News

Far left: Young Asian-Americans danced into the wee hours at a rave at the Bronco Bowl in 1999. The Oak Cliff venue, known for quality concerts, cheap beer and, yes, bowling, closed in 2003 after 42 years in business. HELEN JAU/Dallas Morning News

Health & Education

Decent health care and a good education were hard to come by in 19th-century Dallas. Medical research and training were in their infancy, and patent medicines were popular. The first really modern hospital, St. Paul's, didn't open until 1897. Meanwhile, voters consistently rejected school taxes. Not until 1884 was Dallas able to form a public school district, and from the beginning it was underfunded and overcrowded.

But in the 20th century, Dallas became a leader in both fields. Beginning with the opening of the Texas Baptist Memorial Sanitarium (later renamed Baylor University Hospital) in 1909, Dallas gained more first-rate medical facilities, including two world-renowned institutions devoted to the care of children, Texas Scottish Rite Hospital and Children's Medical Center. Medical education also has flourished. Southwestern Medical College,

launched in 1943 in eight prefabricated buildings near the county hospital, Parkland, soon became part of the University of Texas System. Four of its professors have won Nobel Prizes for Medicine.

The Dallas Independent School District gradually expanded, adding schools in communities throughout Dallas County. The oldest private school still in existence is Ursuline Academy, founded by six Roman Catholic nuns in 1874. Institutions of higher learning were slower to take root. Several early attempts failed before the Methodist church accepted an offer of free acreage for a campus adjacent to the new Highland Park subdivision; Southern Methodist University opened in 1915. Today, Dallas boasts a strong community college system as well as the University of Dallas, University of Texas at Dallas and a local campus of Denton's University of North Texas.

Fifth Year class graduates of Miss Ela Hockaday School for Girls, 1927. Front row: Elizabeth Cleveland, Mary Alice Wren, Kathryn Logue and Sarah Franklin. Back row: Dorothy McCarty, Marion Lege and Jessie Jones. *Natalie and George Lee*

Baylor College of Dentistry/LaDawn Brock

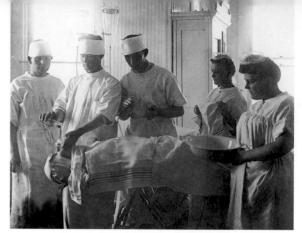

Dorothy Lange (second from right), with a fellow nurse and three doctors, in the operating room at O'Neall Sanitarium, circa 1904.

The Baylor Medical and Dental Band was formed from the Baylor University medical and dental schools, both in Dallas until the medical school moved to Houston in 1944. Both institutions have since separated from Baylor University, but still bear the school's name.

Right: The "Dinky" on Hillcrest Avenue near Southern Methodist University, circa 1915. The line ran from the university to Dallas' streetcar line. Employees were Frank Reedy (left) and "Dad" Johnson, operator.

Opposite: May Forster Smith (right) and Children's Medical Center nurses stood outside the hospital's expanded cottage. A public health nurse who treated children at an open-air clinic on the lawn of the old Parkland Hospital, Smith led the way to start Children's. *Children's Medical Center*

Carol Duff, archives Highland Park United Methodist Church

St. Paul's Hospital laboratory, circa 1930.

Top right: Women shelled peas for the school lunch program in the 1930s.

Right: Neighborhood kids packed Bethany Presbyterian Church Bible school in the early 1930s. It was on Knight Street near Sam Houston Elementary School.

Beverly Littlejohn

Leanor Villareal

St. Ann's schoolchildren assembled for the groundbreaking of the St. Ann's Commercial High School for girls in 1945 in Little Mexico.

Below: The first graduating class of Lincoln High School, 1939 *Kaji Francis Smith*

Texas/Dallas History & Archives Division, Dallas Public Library

Natalie and George Lee

Dallas Country Day School students dressed as Pilgrims for a Thanksgiving pageant in 1945.

Top: Nurses conferred at the Ethel Ransom Memorial Hospital about 1946. Riley Andrew Ransom started the hospital in Gainesville, then moved it to Fort Worth, where he was the first black doctor in Tarrant County. He named the hospital for his wife, a teacher and graduate nurse.

Good Street Baptist Church Community Center served as a clinic for a doctor and nurse and four young patients, about 1952.

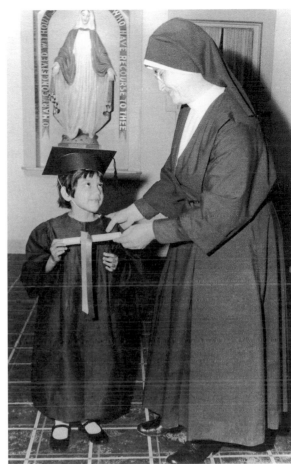

Josie Cantu graduated from kindergarten at St. Ann's School, about 1957.

Left: George Washington Carver Elementary held its African Dance Extravaganza in 1955.
Kay Francis Smith

Opposite: ROTC students stood at attention on the steps of Crozier Tech High School, about 1946. *Nathan L. Gappelberg*

Kay Francis Smith

Kay Francis Smith

Members of the Phi Delta Kappa sorority, an association of educators, met in 1988.

Top right: George Washington Carver Elementary School had nine sets of twins in 1969.

Right: Former New York Giants football player Keith Davis demonstrated his strength in 1997 to Aikin Elementary students in North Dallas by pressing fifth-grade teachers Sandra Moore (left) and Melanie Brooks over his head. Davis taught positive attitudes and habits at schools throughout the area. *LOUIS DeLUCA/Dallas Morning News*

Jane Whitledge adjusted Cletus Bristol's graduation cap before a ceremony to honor the 103-year-old with an honorary high school diploma from Frisco High School at Frisco Senior Center on Oct. 13, 2005. Whitledge, an employee with FISD, discovered Bristol never graduated when interviewing him for a history of Frisco schools.

LARA SOLT/Dallas Morning News

Below: First grader Taylor Kirby (left) laughed at a book as her mother, Yolanda Anderson, read aloud during the annual Warm Up to a Good Book event at the Classical Magnet Elementary School in Richardson in 2003. Also listening to the story were classmates Noele Jenkins (center) and La Desha Ray (barely visible at right). Students and teachers were encouraged to wear pajamas to school for the special reading event. *COURTNEY PERRY/Dallas Morning News*

Below: Second-grader Nikki Burns (left) gathered with her classmates after McKenzie Elementary School students marched around the school and an adjacent park in patriotic recognition of Memorial Day 2003 in Mesquite. At the end of the parade, students joined in saying the Pledge of Allegiance and singing "God Bless America." *COURTNEY PERRY/Dallas Morning News*

Carter High School students chanted Stella McCartney's name during a party in the fashion designer's honor on May 3, 2006, at Neiman Marcus in NorthPark Center.

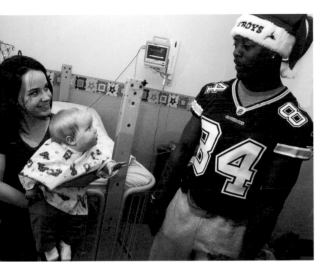

MICHAEL AINSWORTH/Dallas Morning News

Reassured by mom Kristen Pope, 9-month-old Jared Pope stared at receiver Patrick Crayton during the Dallas Cowboys players' and cheerleaders' 20th annual visit to Medical City's Children's Hospital in December 2008.

TOM FOX/Dallas Morning News

Family nurse practitioner Bethany "Beth" McClean got 6-year-old Isaiah Coleman to stick out his tongue during an examination in 2008. The Hurst-Euless-Bedford Independent School District and the JPS Health Network converted a portable classroom into a clinic for children in 2006.

Left: Tharon Robert of Hutchins reached to touch a demonstration doll in an incubator during a 2006 Sibling Support Group class at Parkland Memorial Hospital. The class explained why the tiny infants in the neonatal intensive care unit weren't ready to go home. *LARA SOLT/Dallas Morning News*

Adamson High School students attended a quinceanera on May 31, 2008.

Right top: Carlos Vargas, a 15-year-old sophomore, practiced his cello in 2010 outside a music room at Booker T. Washington High School for the Performing and Visual Arts. The arts magnet school was expanded in 2008, providing more room for the students to pursue music, dance and visual arts in addition to the traditional curriculum.

Right: Michael Hinojosa, superintendent of the Dallas Independent School District, read to children at the J.W. Ray Learning Center as part of Drop Everything and Read in March 2006.

SONYA N. HEBERT/Dallas Morning News

Irelsie Alvarez celebrated with fellow graduates at the conclusion of the 2009 Mesquite Horn High School commencement ceremony at the Garland Special Events Center.

Commerce

The coming of the railroads to Dallas in the 1870s allowed enterprising merchants to import a vast assortment of wares, including furniture, clothing, toys and sporting goods. New jobs, such as sales clerks, were created, and the urban population began to soar. The railroads also encouraged fledgling manufacturers to produce goods for export. Capitalizing on the region's profitable cattle trade, several entrepreneurs began making saddles, harnesses and other equipment. By 1900, Dallas led the world in the manufacture of leather goods. It was the world's largest maker of cotton gins and cotton gin machinery. Cotton was the cash crop, with Dallas being the largest inland cotton market in the world. The area also was fostering a growing millinery and apparel industry.

Its successful bid to become a regional Federal Reserve headquarters in 1914 consolidated Dallas' position as a banking center for the Southwest. In the 1930s, far-sighted bankers took a gamble and made loans to oilmen, accepting untapped reserves as collateral. As a result, Dallas became a business center for the oil industry, with a ripple effect in real estate, luxury retailing and the local service industry.

After World War II, Dallas capitalized on its central geographic location, excellent transportation, low taxes, stable workforce, and supportive political climate to attract new businesses. As a result, by 2000, Dallas was headquarters for some of the nation's largest corporations, and manufacturing employed 14 percent of the workforce, many of those jobs in aeronautics and the high-tech industry.

Wagons loaded with cotton were a common sight on Elm Street starting when the railroads came to Dallas in the 1870s. This photo is from about 1900. *Texas/Dallas History & Archives Division, Dallas Public Library*

The Collections of the Dallas Historical Society

A streetcar traveled down Elm Street in the late 1800s. Streetcars were the main mode of transportation in Dallas starting about then.

Left: Designed for horse-and-buggy traffic, Commerce was one of many streets that had become overburdened with motor traffic by 1913. The city responded by prohibiting parking on Main, Commerce and Elm, which spurred the development of parking garages. Here is the view looking east on Commerce, circa 1885.

Right: John G. Fleming (second from left) and Walter L. Fleming (second from right) opened the John G. Fleming and Sons paper mill in Oak Cliff in 1893. The mill mainly produced egg cartons, cardboard, wallpaper and other building-grade paper, and prospered after other Texas paper mills had failed.

Joseph B. Fleming III

In 1895, Commerce Street was more developed and more congested than it was just 10 years earlier.

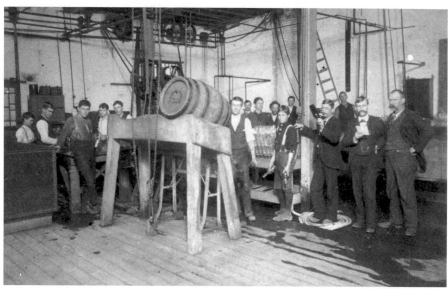

Workers laid railroad tracks in 1900, here looking north on Ervay Street at Commerce Street.

Top right: Henry Schmucker (third from right) checked a bottle in the bottling room of Texas Brewing Co. in Fort Worth. The brewery, begun in the early 1890s, changed its name to Texas Beverage and Cold Storage with the advent of Prohibition in 1918.

Right: Employees ironed customers' clothing in the pressing area of Leachman Laundry in downtown. It opened as Dallas Steam Laundry in 1881. *Manning Shannon*

By 1900, streetcars were becoming increasingly vital to Dallas and new lines were continuing to be laid.

Top left: The first Neiman Marcus store opened in downtown Sept. 10, 1907, in the midst of a nationwide recession. The store, which became an icon for luxury, specialized in high-quality, ready-to-wear clothing at a time when upscale garments generally weren't available off the rack.

Left: Employees of the Dallas Electric Light and Power Co. worked on the lines in 1905. Dallas first got electricity in 1882.

Workers pre-assembled bicycles that arrived in wooden crates in 1914 at the Hans Johnsen Co., 111 N. Akard St. The company, founded by a Danish immigrant in 1901, then delivered the bikes to dealers.

Below right: Store personnel and pilots from Sanger Brothers Air Delivery in Dallas, August 1918. *Texas/Dallas History & Archives Division, Dallas Public Library*

Below: The Nolan Brothers Drug Store, neatly kept in 1915, later became Eagle Drug. *Texas/Dallas History & Archives Division, Dallas Public Library*

Opposite: Employees of A. Zeese Engraving Co. and Electric Automobile Supplies dressed dapperly for a May 1917 photo promoting the International Photo Engravers Union, Local 38. They piled into cars in front of Palace Electric Garage. *Texas/Dallas History & Archives Division, Dallas Public Library*

Francie Johnsen

Texas/Dallas History & Archives Division, Dallas Public Library

DMN Archives

A. H. Belo & Co. directors met Sept. 22, 1925, in George Bannerman Dealey's office just before *The Dallas Morning News'* 40th anniversary. From left: Tom Finty Jr., John F. Lubben, Dealey, his son Walter A. Dealey and Ennis Cargill.

Dr Pepper Snapple Group Inc.

Dr Pepper was invented in 1885 in Waco by Wade Morrison, who co-founded the Artesian Manufacturing and Bottling Co., which later became the Dr Pepper Co. The company's headquarters relocated in 1922 to 401 Main St. on what is now Dealey Plaza.

Top left: Horse-drawn wagons were still common even into the 1920s on Commerce Street in downtown Dallas.

Below: Clifford Johnson (second from left) and other workers supplied tires, tubes and other goods at Isaac's Junk Shop in the 1920s. *Philip Johnson*

Opposite: An aerial view of downtown Dallas on April 7, 1928, showed a booming city. Dallas' population zoomed from 158,976 in 1920 to 260,475 in 1930. *Carol Duff, archives Highland Park United Methodist Church*

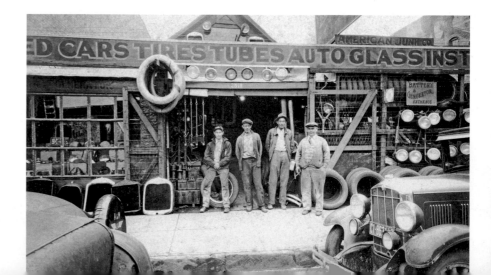

Edgewood Pharmacy offered curbside service in 1927, when car hops generally were male.

Right: Siblings Maria and Filiberto Martinez resided in 1935 in Eagle Ford Village, one of two villages that Southwestern States Portland Cement Co. built to house its employees, most of whom were Mexican immigrants.

Far right: The Tower Petroleum Building, opened in 1931, was noted for its art deco design by Dallas architect Mark Lemmon. He also designed the Museum of Natural History and the Hall of State at Fair Park. *The Collections of the Dallas Historical Society*

In 1927, a Southland Ice Co. employee in Oak Cliff began offering milk, bread and eggs on Sundays and evenings when grocery stores were closed. The idea caught on, and the company eventually became the 7-Eleven chain.

Inspectors stood behind tubs of raw meat in the 1930s, when the city of Dallas began a crackdown on unsanitary conditions.

Below: Harry Kollman and Dick Bordeau were two regulars at the original Dickey's Barbecue Pit when it opened in 1941. The restaurant was on Knox and Henderson. *Dickey's Barbecue Pit*

James LaBarba looked over his cattle on the LaBarba Family Farm about 1945 after a day at work at his business, American Produce and Vegetable Co.

Ernest C. Dillard and newsboys and girls prepared to hit the streets outside Dillard's Variety & Hardware Store about 1947.

Right: South Ervay Street bustled about 1948.

Below: Western Electric Co., part of AT&T, retrained World War II veterans in 1946 for manufacturing and installation work. Its facility was at Ninth Street and Zang Boulevard. *Gene Allen*

Francie Johnsen

Texas/Dallas History & Archives Division, Dallas Public Library

Teenagers listened to records at the H.L. Green variety store, at Main and Ervay, on March 23, 1950.

Top left: Hans Johnsen Co. hosted a Schwinn sales meeting in 1953. Howard R. Johnsen is on the far right.

Left: Peggy Mayne of Grand Saline, Texas, sold tomatoes from the back of her truck in 1951 at the Dallas Farmers Market. Farmers have sold fresh produce since the late 1800s at the site, officially sanctioned as a city-owned and -operated market in 1941. *Texas/Dallas History & Archives Division, Dallas Public Library*

Texas/Dallas History & Archives Division, Dallas Public Library

Bailey Gilmore marked price changes sent via ticker tape to one of the many chalkboards where commodity prices were posted in the trading hall at the Cotton Exchange in 1951. Dallas was one of the world's largest cotton markets in the 1940s.

Nina F. Guerrero Rivera

Antonio Rivera was a familiar sight in downtown Dallas for more than 26 years. He sold *The Dallas Morning News* and *The Daily Times Herald* at two different corners. Here he is at the corner of Elm and Akard about 1950.

Left: Inspectors examined raw and bagged cotton at the Cotton Exchange in 1963.

Texas/Dallas History & Archives Division, Dallas Public Library

Opposite: Cotton trailers converged outside the Forney Cotton Gin, one of the last gins in the area, in 1958.

Texas/Dallas History & Archives Division, Dallas Public Library

Vought Aeronautics in Grand Prairie in 1973 represented the area's strong defense industry.

Right: Never-completed condos on Bobtown Road in Garland were bulldozed in 1987, casualties of the savings-and-loan bust that ravaged the Texas economy. *DMN Archives*

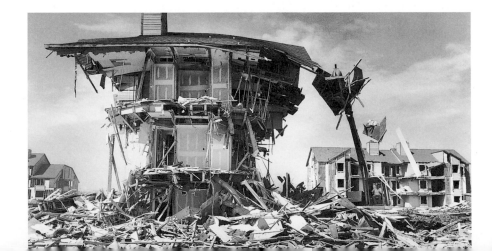

RANDY GROTHE/Dallas Morning News

In 1988, Robert Crandall, head of American Airlines, was considered an industry leader as a promoter of the hub system, in which flights from small airports converged at large ones such as Dallas/Fort Worth International Airport for connections.

Left: Herb Kelleher, Southwest Airlines' colorful chairman known for chain smoking, guffaws and kisses, donned the captain's hat for takeoff from Love Field in 1991. *DAVID WOO/Dallas Morning News*

RICHARD MICHAEL PRUITT/Dallas Morning News

Truck frames moved along the assembly line at the General Motors assembly plant in Arlington in 2002. The factory began operating in 1954.

Right: The Nortel campus was among the technology companies making up Telecom Corridor in Richardson. The telecom industry boomed in the late 1990s, only to crash in the early 2000s, putting many out of work.

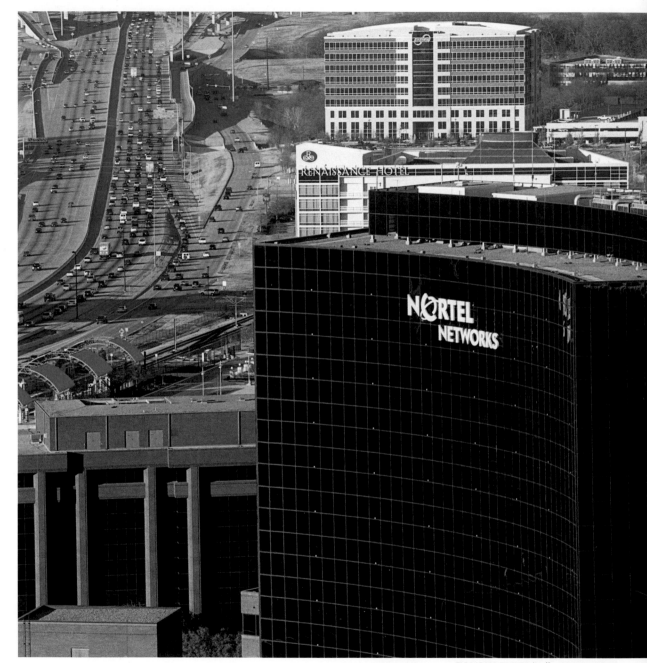

DAMON WINTER/Dallas Morning News

Legendary Realtor Ebby Halliday, 99, got an autographed team ball from Dallas Maverick Dirk Nowitzki at halftime in an NBA game against the Sacramento Kings on March 5, 2010.

Madeline Stone drove a tractor, plowing the fields of her 30-acre farm west of Celina in 2004.

Left: Norman Brinker (right) and executive chef Lex Berlin grilled up vegetables at the Macaroni Grill in Addison in 1992. Brinker popularized casual dining with chains including Steak and Ale, Chili's, Bennigan's and On the Border. DAVID WOO/ Dallas Morning News

Sports

Dallas residents were as sports-minded in 1885 as they are now. A mania for roller skating and bicycling swept the city, and lawn tennis, croquet and golf soon followed. All of these sports appealed to women as much as to men.

Organized team sports, especially baseball and football, were just beginning to play fixed schedules against rival communities. From 1888 through 1958, Dallas fielded a team in the Texas League under a variety of names. Fifteen times the Dallas Hams, Giants, Submarines, Steers, Rebels or Eagles either finished the regular season atop the standings or won the post-season playoffs.

Football allegiance originally focused on high school and college teams. Southern Methodist University sent a team to the Rose Bowl in 1935.

Then, in the late 1940s, Doak Walker led the SMU Mustangs to consecutive Southwest Conference championships and won the 1948 Heisman Trophy, making him the first athlete to receive it in his junior year. In the early 1960s, two professional teams, the Dallas Texans and the Dallas Cowboys, competed for fans until Lamar Hunt moved the Texans to Kansas City in 1963, leaving the Cowboys to emerge as "America's Team."

Today, Dallas is home to professional basketball and ice hockey teams and the annual Byron Nelson golf tournament. Dallas has even hosted a Grand Prix auto race and World Cup soccer matches. As they have for the past 125 years, sporting activities provide a focus for local boosterism, while serving as a bond for an increasingly diverse population.

Texas Stadium became a sea of white as fans were encouraged to wear something white to the game between the Dallas Cowboys and the New York Giants in the second round of the playoffs on Jan. 13, 2008, at Texas Stadium in Irving. *TOM FOX/Dallas Morning News*

Tom Monagan, who competed on his high-wheel bicycle, was captain of the Dallas Wheel Club in 1887.

Right: Both men and women were members of a lawn tennis club in the late 1800s. *The Collections of the Dallas Historical Society*

The Dallas Hams were Dallas' earliest professional baseball team, formed in 1888. In keeping with baseball's rough reputation at the time, the team's office was in a saloon.

Manning Shannon

C.F. and Susan Carter show their catch of the day in front of their home on Ross Avenue in Dallas, circa 1900. These fish were caught at the Fin and Feather Club.

Below right: Dallas High School football team, 1902. *DMN Archives*

Below: Downtown Dallas' first indoor swimming pool, known as "Cascade Plunge," was part of the Leachman Laundry about 1920. *Manning Shannon*

The Collections of the Dallas Historical Society

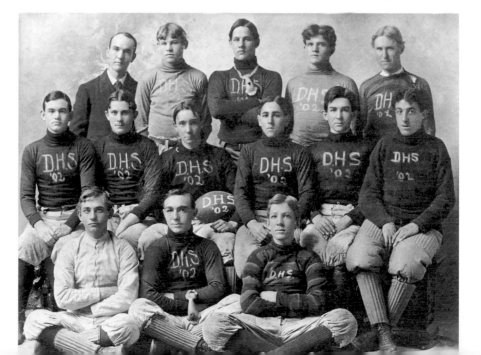

Above: Dr. Norman Washington Harllee (back row, center) was both the Booker T. Washington High School principal and the coach for the school's 1909 Bulldogs football team. He was the first person to have a Dallas school named after him while he was still living.

Hardware merchant Huey & Philp sponsored an amateur baseball club, pictured at Fair Park in 1915.

Guadalupe Rivera Family

On the front page, Jan. 17, 1972: The Cowboys win their first Super Bowl.

Top right: A soccer team sponsored by CAFF won the Catann Allen Trophy during the 1933-34 season. The photo was taken near Oak Lawn Avenue and Turtle Creek Boulevard.

Right: Brad Bradley (from left), Doak Walker and Bradley's father-in-law, Jim Laughead, at Southern Methodist University in 1947. *DMN Archives*

After catching the "Hail Mary" pass, Dallas Cowboys wide receiver Drew Pearson (88) looked back to see the referee signal a touchdown. Quarterback Roger Staubach threw the pass in a last-ditch — and successful — effort to win their playoff game Jan. 8, 1975, at Metropolitan Stadium in Minneapolis.

On the front page, Jan. 16, 1978: The Cowboys beat Denver in Super Bowl XII.

Right: Super Bowl XII MVPs Randy White (54) and Harvey Martin hailed the Cowboys' victory over Denver in 1978. *LARRY PROVART/Dallas Morning News*

Texas Rangers pitcher Nolan Ryan pitched his seventh career no-hitter on May 1, 1991, against Toronto.

Top left: The stands of the Cotton Bowl were filled with 75,587 fans for the 1983 football game between the University of Texas and the University of Oklahoma.

Left: Dallas Mavericks player Sam Perkins went for the basketball in a January 1986 game at Reunion Arena. *LOUIS DeLUCA/Dallas Morning News*

Nolan Ryan and Pudge Rodriguez scuffled with Chicago White Sox hitter Robin Ventura, who charged the mound at the Ballpark in Arlington in 1993.

Below: Golf legend Byron Nelson greeted Tiger Woods, then 16 and taking the golf circuit by storm, at Hole 6 in 1992 at the Four Seasons TPC at Las Colinas.

JUDY WALGREN/
Dallas Morning News

On the front page, Feb. 1, 1993: The Cowboys win another Super Bowl.

BRAD LOPER/The Arlington News

SUPER BOWL XXVIII SPECIAL SECTION, PAGES 1-20B.

The Dallas Morning News

BACK-TO-BACK CHAMPS

Strong 2nd half carries Cowboys to 30-13 win over Bills

On the front page, Jan. 31, 1994: For the second year, the Cowboys win over Buffalo in the Super Bowl.

DAVID WOO/Dallas Morning News

Rangers pitcher Kenny Rogers waved to fans after pitching a perfect game in 1994.

Left: The opening ceremonies of the World Cup were held in the Cotton Bowl June 17, 1994. *IRWIN THOMPSON/Dallas Morning News*

IRWIN THOMPSON/Dallas Morning News

Emmitt Smith (from left), "Bullet" Bob Hayes and Michael Irvin held aloft the NFC Championship trophy in 1996.

On the front page, Jan. 29, 1996: The Cowboys win a third Super Bowl.

WILLIAM SNYDER/Dallas Morning News

Coach Barry Switzer got a Gatorade bath after the Dallas Cowboys beat the Pittsburgh Steelers on Jan. 28, 1996, in Super Bowl XXX.

SMILEY N. POOL/Dallas Morning News

A composite image tracked the movement of Olympic gold medalist Carly Patterson through her signature dismount, the double Arabian, in 2004 at the World Olympic Gymnastics Academy in Plano.

IRWIN THOMPSON/Dallas Morning News

MICHAEL MULVEY/Dallas Morning News

DAVID WOO/Dallas Morning News

Although often at odds, NBA commissioner David Stern (left) and Mavericks owner Mark Cuban chatted pleasantly in the 2000 preseason.

Drivers John Andretti (43) and Rick Mast (75) escaped their cars after a pileup April 5, 1998, on Turn 1 in the first minutes of the Winston Cup race at Texas Motor Speedway in Fort Worth.

Top center: Mike Modano hoisted the Stanley Cup after the Stars stuck it to the Buffalo Sabres in the third overtime of Game 6 for the ice hockey championship in 1999.

Right: Brett Hull shot the goal that won the Stanley Cup. *LOUIS DeLUCA/Dallas Morning News*

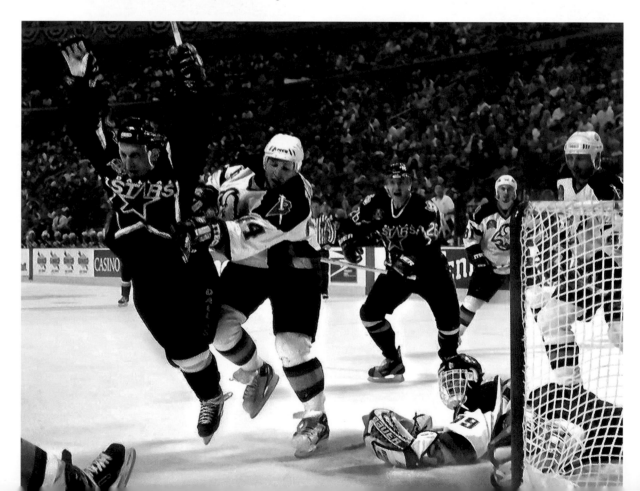

LOUIS DeLUCA/Dallas Morning News

IRWIN THOMPSON/Dallas Morning News

TOM FOX/Arlington Morning News

In 2002, Cowboys running back Emmitt Smith set the all-time rushing record, eclipsing Walter Payton's previous mark.

Top left: Texas Rangers catcher Ivan "Pudge" Rodriguez and third baseman Todd Zeile celebrated winning the American League West Division in 1999.

Left: Race horses thundered out of the starting gate for the Premier race at Lone Star Park in Grand Prairie in 2003.

Bryce Buford drenched Southlake Carroll High School coach Todd Dodge in Gatorade in the closing seconds of their 5A Division II championship at Texas Stadium in 2005.

Below: Dallas Mavericks owner Mark Cuban held the trophy aloft in Game 6 of the NBA Western Conference Finals against the Phoenix Suns in 2006.

TOM FOX/Dallas Morning News

LOUIS DeLUCA/Dallas Morning News

Dirk Nowitzki got a ride from Mavericks teammate Michael Finley in 2003 after defeating the Sacramento Kings in Game 7 of the NBA Western Conference semifinals.

Below: Bareback bronc rider Royce Ford of Hudson, Colo., took a first-place ride on Take It Back during the Fort Worth Stock Show & Rodeo on Feb. 2, 2005. *TOM FOX/Dallas Morning News*

Opposite: The green flag drops on the start of the NASCAR Nextel Cup Series Dickies 500 race at the Texas Motor Speedway, Nov. 4, 2007.

TOM FOX/Dallas Morning News

VERNON BRYANT/Dallas Morning News

Texas freshman QB Colt McCoy (12) gave thanks for the Longhorns' win at the end of the Red River Shootout between the University of Texas and the University of Oklahoma at the Cotton Bowl in Dallas on Oct. 7, 2006. Texas beat Oklahoma 28-10.

TOM FOX/Dallas Morning News

TOM FOX/Dallas Morning News

Manny Pacquiao celebrated his welterweight title fight win over Joshua Clottey on March 13, 2010, at Cowboys Stadium in Arlington.

Top left: University of Oklahoma fan Angie Nelson (right) of Dallas taunted University of Texas fan Jeff Shamburger of Tyler after OU scored a touchdown to tie the score at 14 in the Red River Shootout at the Cotton Bowl in 2007. She was one of the few OU fans sitting on the UT side.

Left: The Dallas Cowboys Cheerleaders, shown here in 2008, have been an America's Team icon since adopting star-spangled uniforms in 1972. *TOM FOX/Dallas Morning News*

From the dugout, the Rangers watch the action at an exhibition game between their team and the Kansas City Royals during spring training March 5, 2010, in Surprise, Ariz.

Right: Rangers right fielder Vladimir Guerrero missed the long fly that went for a triple in the ninth inning of the Rangers' 2-1 loss to the Minnesota Twins in Minneapolis on May 28, 2010.

An American flag and a Texas flag are unfurled for the pre-game ceremonies and National Anthem before the Texas Rangers home opener against the Toronto Blue Jays at Rangers Ballpark in Arlington on April 5, 2010.

Top 25 Events

What are the most important events in a city's history? Simply put, ones that have the greatest long-term impact. The historians who compiled this list of "Top 25 Events" unanimously ranked the coming of the railroads in the 1870s as No. 1. Becoming the first rail crossroads in North Texas made all subsequent development possible. Later transportation links — highways, airports and mass transit — logically also scored high.

A good transportation network encouraged publishing, banking and the high-tech industry to flourish here. Effective government, culture, sports, and the 1936 Texas Centennial Exposition (when Dallas gained the nickname "Big D") also shaped the city.

Though President John F. Kennedy's assassination was tragic and left an enduring imprint on the city's psyche, it may not have had as lasting an impact on Dallas as some other events. But it did galvanize city leaders into being more inclusive and led to a host of civic improvements through Goals for Dallas, which is why it ranks in the top half of the list.

Darwin Payne,
Dallas historian, professor emeritus of communications at Southern Methodist University

Michael V. Hazel,
editor of *Legacies* regional history journal, Dallas historian

Jackie McElhaney,
Dallas historian

Carol Roark,
manager Texas/Dallas History & Archives Division, Dallas Public Library

Dr. Robert B. Fairbanks,
professor of urban history and chairman of the Department of History, University of Texas at Arlington

Judith Garrett Segura,
retired president of the Belo Foundation and Belo historian

No. 1

Railroads and telegraphs arrive, 1872-73.

The Collections of the Dallas Historical Society

On the front page, April 5, 1886: Dallas is declared "the Greatest Railway City of the Southwest."

The arrival of the railroads in 1872 and 1873 was the key event in the development of Dallas, rapidly turning the city into a boomtown. Railroads gave farmers an outlet for their products and enabled merchants to import manufactured goods. By 1890, Dallas had become the largest city in Texas.

107

No. 2

Dallas/Fort Worth International Airport opens, 1974.

JOE LAIRD/Dallas Morning News

Dallas Mayor Wes Wise (left) and Fort Worth Mayor R.M. Stovall (right) greeted Dr. J.W. Parker and his wife, Patricia, the first passengers to step off a plane at D/FW Jan. 12, 1974.

Right: An American Airlines jet takes off as a storm approaches the control tower at D/FW Sept. 11, 2006.

TOM FOX/Dallas Morning News

No. 3

George Kessler develops the first city plan, which shapes Dallas for years, 1911.

Far right: Union Station, opened in 1916, was the centerpiece of a civic gateway envisioned for Dallas by city planner George Kessler.

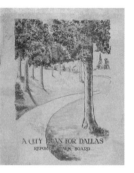

A CITY PLAN FOR DALLAS
REPORT PARK BOARD

On the front page, June 29, 1911: Kessler meets with Dallas officials.

The cover of Kessler's 1912 plan.

No. 4

Dallas is selected as the county seat, 1850.

DMN Archives

A new brick courthouse (above), shown in 1857, replaced the two-room log courthouse in 1855. Because all county legal business was conducted here, businesses sprouted up around the courthouse and helped fuel Dallas' growth.

DMN Archives

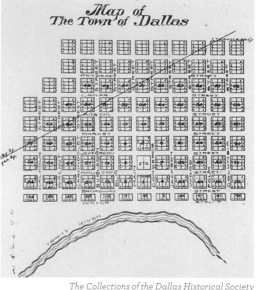
The Collections of the Dallas Historical Society

John Neely Bryan's 1844 map of Dallas.

Left: The Old Red Courthouse in an undated photo was constructed in 1892 on the spot where the first one used to be. It was Dallas' sixth courthouse. It has undergone many transformations through the years, but is now the Old Red Museum of Dallas County History & Culture.

No. 5

Dallas is selected as the site for the 11th District of the Federal Reserve Bank, 1914.

On the front page, Nov. 17, 1914: The Federal Reserve's opening is celebrated.

The lobby of the old Federal Reserve building on Akard Street. Being chosen as the site for the bank was a major achievement for Dallas.

DMN Archives

111

No. 6

The Texas Centennial Exposition is held, 1936.

On the front page, June 6, 1936: The exposition begins.

The nightly light show at the 1936 Texas Centennial Exposition — with enough wattage to power a city of 100,000 — turned the Esplanade of State into an ever-changing spectacle.

The Collections of the Dallas Historical Society

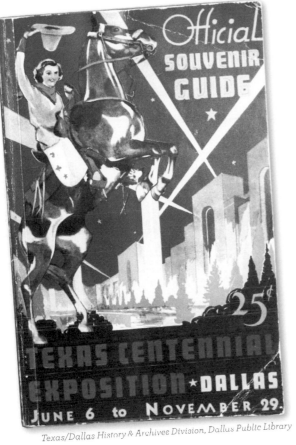

An official program from the spectacular celebration of Texas' 100th anniversary of independence.

Right: More than 6 million visitors from every state and throughout the world stepped through the entrance to Fair Park in 1936 to visit the exposition, which lasted six months.

No. 7

The Dallas Morning News is founded, 1885.

The composing room of *The News,* about 1886.

Below: *The News* used a Bullock press to produce its first edition. And George Bannerman Dealey (far right) began his long career as not only a Dallas newspaperman, but also as a promoter of the city. *DMN Archives*

DMN Archives

On the front page, Oct. 1, 1885: The newspaper's historic first edition.

Edward M. "Ted" Dealey (from left), Joe Dealey, George Bannerman Dealey and James M. Moroney in the pressroom of *The News* on April 9, 1942.

No. 8

Love Field is constructed, 1917.

Texas/Dallas History & Archives Division, Dallas Public Library

Love Field, shown in 1925, converted to civilian use in 1927.

Texas/Dallas History & Archives Division, Dallas Public Library

In 1940, 200,000 travelers passed through the airport, then the seventh-busiest in the nation.

Inside *The News*, Nov. 11, 1917:
Training begins at Love Field.

Pilots, including Edward Duff (standing, third from left) at Love Field, about 1920. They flew planes with OX-5 rotary engines known as "Jennys."

No. 9

Residents approve the council-manager form of municipal government, 1930.

BOB W. SMITH/Dallas Morning News

On the front page, Oct. 11, 1930: The proposal passes by roughly 4,500 votes.

The Dallas City Council at work on Oct. 5, 1968.

No. 10

Texas Instruments' transistors begin to establish the company as a worldwide electronics powerhouse, 1954.

Howdy, Folks!..

..your new neighbor on these 300 acres is

TEXAS INSTRUMENTS
INCORPORATED

here we GROW again!

Texas Instruments Inc.

Texas Instruments, shown here in March 1957, is now largely focused on making chips for cellphones and other wireless devices. It was the first company to develop production techniques for the transistor radio. TI's Jack Kilby, inventor of the integrated circuit, was on the team that produced what became the first handheld calculator in 1967.

On the front page, May 1, 1954: TI starts churning out silicon transistors.

Left: The first handheld calculator was huge by today's standards. *Texas Instruments Inc.*

No. 11

Voters approve the creation of DART as the regional transportation system, 1983.

April 23, 2008, was the first official morning of commuter traffic on the new Dallas Area Rapid Transit System. Passengers awaited the train at the Westmoreland station. *LOUIS DeLUCA/ Dallas Morning News*

President John F. Kennedy is assassinated, 1963.

WALT SISCO/Dallas Morning News

On the front page, Nov. 23, 1963: The tragedy is chronicled.

The presidential motorcade traveled along Main Street shortly before the assassination on Nov. 22, 1963.

No. 13

Desegregation of public schools and public facilities begins, 1961.

RICHARD MICHAEL PRUITT/Dallas Morning News

On the front page, Sept. 7, 1961: School desegregation is the top story.

In 1977, a Lakewood Elementary teacher directed a child to the right bus during the desegregation era.

No. 14

Construction begins on Central Expressway, among the first modern freeways, 1947.

Texas/Dallas History & Archives Division, Dallas Public Library

Central Expressway was built on the former right of way of the Houston & Texas Central Railway.

Right: The expressway today, looking south from Haskell Avenue. Cityplace tower is on the left.

DAVID WOO/Dallas Morning News

No. 15

Drought inspires far-reaching plans for an adequate municipal water supply, 1950s.

Farmers Jim Martin (left) and John McCroan discussed crop damage caused by the June 1953 heat wave. A catastrophic drought in the 1950s resulted in long-range planning to meet the city's water needs.

On the front page, Dec. 11, 1956: Residents will vote on water plans.

Texas/Dallas History & Archives Division, Dallas Public Library

CLINT GRANT/Dallas Morning News

Several dry spells struck in the 1970s, but they were less severe than the catastrophic drought that parched the state in the 1950s. Here, a Cedar Hill cornfield was in need of rain in July 1974.

No. 16

The State Fair of Texas is organized, 1886-87.

DMN Archives

The Collections of the Dallas Historical Society

DMN Archives

The Texas State Fair opened in 1886. A day later, the Dallas State Fair and Exposition opened. The rival organizations merged the following year, forming the Texas State Fair and Dallas Exposition. Above, a view of the grounds in 1900. Top left, visitors wandered the fair in 1890. Left, a poster from the same year advertised the fair.

No. 17

The North American Aviation plant opens, bringing the aviation industry to Dallas, 1941.

CLINT GRANT/Dallas Morning News

A Canadair Challenger was readied for refurbishing on July 25, 1978.

DMN Archives

The first A-7B versions of the Corsair II Navy fighter started down an assembly line at Ling-Temco-Vought's Grand Prairie plant in 1967.

Inside *The News*, April 6, 1941: Work on the aviation plant nears completion.

This is the last B-36 Peacemaker produced in the Convair factory in Fort Worth in 1954. Only four of the world's first intercontinental bombers survive today.

No. 18

Dallas Citizens Council forms, 1937.

Texas/Dallas History & Archives Division, Dallas Public Library

On the front page, March 2, 1938: The Dallas Citizens Council holds it first meeting.

A Dallas Chamber of Commerce-Dallas Citizens Council joint committee toured a slum a mile from downtown in 1950. The tour led toward the creation of Hamilton Park. Since its founding in 1937, the Dallas Citizens Council has been and remains the most influential civic body in the city.

No. 19

The 14-1 City Council system is instituted, 1991.

KEN GEIGER/Dallas Morning News

Minorities were long underrepresented on the City Council. So civil rights leader Al Lipscomb (left) and 17 others filed a federal suit, which ultimately resulted in the court-ordered election system of 14 single-member districts and an at-large mayor. Steve Bartlett (right) was mayor from 1991 to 1995.

Right: Veteran civil rights activist Roy Williams was the chief plaintiff in the 1988 lawsuit, which began years of court battles, protests and referendums designed to increase minority representation on the City Council.

EVANS CAGLAGE/Dallas Morning News

No. 20

Oak Cliff becomes the first of many annexations in the 20th century, increasing the size of Dallas, 1903.

DMN Archives

Inside *The News*, March 8, 1904: A court decision makes Oak Cliff part of Dallas.

Oak Cliff fended off several annexation attempts by Dallas, but in 1903, the community's depressed economy finally spurred a successful vote to join. Jefferson Boulevard in Oak Cliff, about 1949.

No. 21

Southern Methodist University is founded, 1911.

On the front page, Feb. 5, 1911: Dallas lands SMU.

SMU was founded in 1911, but began operating in 1915. Its first faculty included two Rhodes Scholars. Dallas Hall, the first building on campus, is shown here in the 1920s.

SMU Archives

No. 22

Southwestern Medical School (now UT Southwestern Medical Center) opens, 1943.

On the front page, July 2, 1943: The medical school opens.

For its first 13 years, Southwestern Medical School was housed in World War II army barracks called "the Shacks" on the grounds of the old Parkland Hospital at Maple and Oak Lawn. The tiny wartime medical college is now the University of Texas Southwestern Medical Center, renowned for research and training.

UT Southwestern Medical Center

No. 23

The Dallas Cowboys professional football team forms, 1960.

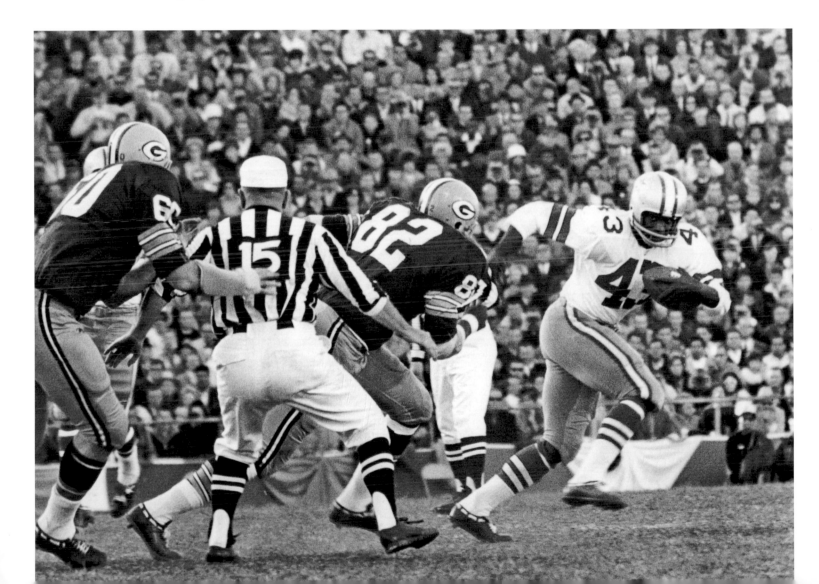

The NFL championship game between the Green Bay Packers and Dallas Cowboys at the Cotton Bowl, Jan. 1, 1967. *DMN Archives*

(continued) *The Dallas Cowboys professional football team forms, 1960.*

DMN Archives

Quarterback Roger Staubach, who guided the team to four NFC titles and two Super Bowl championships, went over strategy with coach Tom Landry.

Right: Coach Landry, general manager Tex Schramm and player personnel chief Gil Brandt built the Cowboys into a winning franchise.

Far right: Staubach turned upfield against the Philadelphia Eagles in 1974.

DMN Archives

DMN Archives

No. 24

The Dallas Public Library opens, following a campaign by the Dallas Federation of Women's Clubs, 1901.

On the front page, Oct. 30, 1901: Thousands attend the library's opening.

The circulation desk of Dallas' first public library, the Carnegie Library, began checking out books on Oct. 29, 1901.

Texas/Dallas History & Archives Division, Dallas Public Library

No. 25

The Arts District is completed, 2009.

TOM FOX/*Dallas Morning News*

On the front page, Oct. 13, 2009: The AT&T Performing Arts Center receives raves.

The Nasher Sculpture Center, which opened in 2003, was created to house Raymond and Patsy Nasher's renowned collection and is one of the few institutions worldwide devoted to the exhibition, study and preservation of modern sculpture. *Walking to the Sky*, a stainless steel and fiberglass sculpture, is a stunning example.

The red drum of the Margot and Bill Winspear Opera House glowed as the AT&T Performing Arts Center was readied for a series of grand opening ceremonies.

Big Tex (above) loomed over the Dallas Grand Prix, a Formula One race held July 8, 1984. Just as automobiles replaced horses on Dallas streets, they also replaced the beasts on the State Fair of Texas racetrack (opposite).

Then & Now

Photographs capture people, places, and events with a clarity and immediacy impossible to match with words. Comparing a historic image to a modern one often evokes a variety of emotions.

Some then-and-now photos provide a reassuring sense of continuity. The Roman Catholic cathedral in downtown Dallas looks much the same as it did when dedicated in 1902, except that its spires were finally completed in time for its 100th anniversary. Dallas Hall is still the stately centerpiece of Southern Methodist University's campus, though now it is flanked by buildings and the vegetation has matured. The view north along Harwood past the Scottish Rite Cathedral has changed since the 1920s, but the cathedral has been lovingly preserved.

Other then-and-now pictures document dramatic change. A tiny opera house on Commerce Street burned in the early 1900s; today Dallas has the impressive architectural gem, the Winspear Opera House. The first Temple Emanu-El on Field and Commerce streets is long gone; since 1957 the congregation has worshipped in a Howard Meyer-designed building in North Dallas. The early wood-frame Parkland Hospital was replaced in 1913 by a brick structure recently restored by a private business. Today, Parkland is part of a huge medical complex that includes UT Southwestern Medical School and several other hospitals.

Comparing old and new photographs can provide dramatic evidence of a city's growth. Contrasting early photos of bare highways with modern shots of dense development reveals the foresight that planners had. Comparing decades-old photos of Love Field and Dallas/Fort Worth International Airport with those taken today are just as telling.

Two photos of *Dallas Morning News* buildings evoke all of these reactions. Only blocks away from the 1885 structure, the current headquarters houses radically different technologies and a vastly expanded mission, yet the newspaper itself represents the continuity of 125 years in Dallas.

North Central Expressway at Northwest Highway was essentially a clean slate in the 1950s. Photographed today from almost the same vantage point (opposite), the interchange teems with traffic and development. NorthPark Center is on the left.

SQUIRE HASKINS/Dallas Morning News

The Dallas diocese was established in 1890, and Sacred Heart was designated its cathedral. The Catholic parish soon outgrew it, and a new building at Ross and Pearl streets was dedicated in 1902. Here parishioners gathered for the consecration of Bishop Patrick Lynch on July 11, 1911. The cathedral (opposite) was renamed Cathedral Santuario de Guadalupe (the Cathedral Shrine of Our Lady of Guadalupe) in 1976. Today it is home to the second-largest cathedral congregation in the U.S. and the largest Latino congregation.

Inwood Village Shopping Center (top), opened in 1949 and shown here in 1952, was North Texas' first big retail center with all-glass storefronts. The center, at Lovers Lane and Inwood Road, got a facelift after new investors bought it in 2003. The theater spire (far right) remains in this 2010 photograph (above).

TOM DILLARD/Dallas Morning News

Known by its dome, Dallas Hall (left) was the first building constructed at Southern Methodist University, which opened in 1915. Dallas Hall (above) is no longer the only building on campus.

SMU Archives

Construction was under way in 1973 at Dallas/Fort Worth International Airport (opposite), which opened the next year and became the world's largest airport in land area. Its price tag was more than $700 million. This current view (top left) looks north at D/FW, which has 174 gates and seven runways. On average last year, almost 154,000 passengers a day arrived at or departed from its terminals.

Park Cities Bank and Trust Co., Dallas, Texas, Heritage Series

DAVID WOO/Dallas Morning News

Traffic could be busy on Preston Road in 1941 (above), even though the area wasn't as built up as it is today. The view today (above right) from the same vantage point — just north of Lovers Lane — shows a considerably different skyline. But the traffic isn't much different.

The Collections of the Dallas Historical Society

DAVID WOO/Dallas Morning News

The first Jewish temple in North Texas, Temple Emanu-El was founded in 1875 by 11 men, including Alex Sanger of Sanger Brothers fame. This first building (above left), a Moorish Revival style, was erected in 1876 at Field and Commerce streets. The temple moved to its current location (above right), on Hillcrest and Northwest Highway, in 1957. Now about 2,600 families are members.

Texas/Dallas History & Archives Division, Dallas Public Library

DAVID WOO/Dallas Morning News

Carol T. Powers

DAVID WOO/Dallas Morning News

The Triple Underpass (above left), under construction in 1935, was built as a grand entrance to Dallas. George Bannerman Dealey rode in the first car through it in 1936. A similar view today (above) shows the Old Red Museum of Dallas County History & Culture, housed in the 1892 courthouse, shown in the upper right.

The old Federal Reserve Bank on Akard Street (far left), was replaced by this building on Pearl Street (left), just north of downtown and the Dallas Arts District.

The 1920s view north along Harwood Street shows the Scottish Rite Cathedral, which was completed in 1913, and the new Dallas Gas Co. building (on the left).

The cathedral today, also looking north on Harwood Street, was constructed by a group of Scottish Rite Masons at a cost of $300,000.

Crowds on the east bank, across from the Commerce Street bridge, gaped at the rising Trinity River. George Bannerman Dealey was a strong backer of the 1926 project to create a series of levees and redirect the river, which helped minimize damage from flooding in later years. Heavy rains pushed water over the banks and flooded part of the Sylvan Avenue bridge (above right) on Sept. 14, 2009.

The YMCA Dallas opened its first building in 1899 at Commerce and Jackson streets (above left). Its mission was to provide young men with housing, Bible classes, social events, and wellness through spirituality and fitness. The T. Boone Pickens YMCA (above right) in downtown has 23 branches and two camps, Camp Grady Spruce and Collin County Adventure Camp.

Love Field began as an Army flying field in 1917 just southeast of Bachman Lake. It was named after 1st Lt. Moss Lee Love, who died in an airplane crash in San Diego, Calif. Several years later the airport opened to civilian use and in 1928 the city purchased the airfield. Today, Love Field (below) is undergoing extensive improvements, including replacing its terminal and gates.

DAVID WOO/Dallas Morning News

TOM DILLARD/Dallas Morning News

In 1885, *The Dallas Morning News'* first location was on Commerce, between Austin and Lamar. A prominent local banker erected the building, which was designed by Dallas architect Herbert M. Greene. The newspaper's current Young Street building (opposite), which was dedicated in 1949, was built by architect George Dahl and cost $6 million.

The original Parkland Hospital (below left), which opened in 1894, was a wood-frame building constructed on a 17-acre wooded tract on the city's northern edge. In 1954, Parkland moved to its current location (below right), about a mile from the original site on Harry Hines Boulevard. More than 60 percent of area doctors have had training at the hospital, which will get a new 17-story building by 2014. *Dallas Public Library (below left) DAVID WOO/Dallas Morning News (below right)*

DMN Archives

DAVID WOO/Dallas Morning News

7-Eleven Inc. Archives

DAVID WOO/Dallas Morning News

The Southland Ice Co., at 12th and Edgefield in north Oak Cliff (far left), pioneered the convenience store concept. In 1946, the company renamed its stores 7-Eleven to promote extended hours. This store, on Colorado and Zang (left), is a mile from the first icehouse.

The Dallas Opera House (above) opened Oct. 15, 1883, on St. Paul and Main streets with a production of Gilbert and Sullivan's *Iolanthe*. At the opening of the Margot and Bill Winspear Opera House (opposite) on Oct. 17, 2009, partygoers mingled before the Act III Gala.

OSCAR DURAND/Dallas Morning News

A shot, probably taken from atop the Old Red Courthouse (below left), looked east over downtown. The Bank of America building is framed through the courthouse's bell tower (below right) in 2010. *Texas/Dallas History & Archives Division, Dallas Public Library (below left) DAVID WOO/Dallas Morning News (below right)*

Index

DAVID WOO/Dallas Morning News

In 2010, some employees gathered in front of *The Dallas Morning News* building on Young Street (above), and outside of the North Plant in Plano (left), where the newspaper is printed. The North Plant, which began operating in 1985, at the corner of Plano Parkway and Coit Road, is 17 miles from the downtown building. *DAVID WOO/Dallas Morning News*

ACKNoWLEDGE THE RIGHT OF THE PEOPLE TO GET FROM THE NEWSPAPER BOTH SIDES OF EVERY IMPORTANT QUESTION

G. B. DEALEY

The Dallas Morning News

EVANS CAGLAGE/Dallas Morning News

Some of the employees who worked in *The Dallas Morning News* building downtown in 2010 posed for a group shot. Founder George Bannerman Dealey wanted architect George Dahl to construct a building that would "add to the beauty of the plaza in front of us and in no way detract from it."